Antarctic Shag

by Grace Hansen

Abdo Kids Jumbo is an Imprint of Abdo Kids
abdobooks.com

abdobooks.com

Published by Abdo Kids, a division of ABDO, P.O. Box 398166, Minneapolis, Minnesota 55439.
Copyright © 2022 by Abdo Consulting Group, Inc. International copyrights reserved in all countries.
No part of this book may be reproduced in any form without written permission from the publisher.
Abdo Kids Jumbo™ is a trademark and logo of Abdo Kids.

Printed in the United States of America, North Mankato, Minnesota.

102021

012022

Photo Credits: Alamy, Getty Images, iStock, Shutterstock

Production Contributors: Teddy Borth, Jennie Forsberg, Grace Hansen
Design Contributors: Candice Keimig, Victoria Bates

Library of Congress Control Number: 2021940119
Publisher's Cataloging-in-Publication Data

Names: Hansen, Grace, author.

Title: Antarctic shag / by Grace Hansen

Description: Minneapolis, Minnesota : Abdo Kids, 2022 | Series: Antarctic animals | Includes online
    resources and index.

Identifiers: ISBN 9781098209384 (lib. bdg.) | ISBN 9781098260095 (ebook) | ISBN 9781098260446
    (Read-to-Me ebook)

Subjects: LCSH: Shag (Bird)--Juvenile literature. | Imperial shag--Juvenile literature. | Cormorants--
    Juvenile literature. | Birds--Behavior--Arctic regions--Juvenile literature. | Zoology--Antarctica--
    Juvenile literature. | Antarctica--Juvenile literature.

Classification: DDC 591.709113--dc23

Table of Contents

Antarctica

Antarctica is the southernmost continent. Nearly all of Antarctica is covered by ice. It is one of the coldest, driest, and windiest places on Earth. But some amazing animals still live there!

Africa
South America
Antarctica
South Pole
Australia

Antarctic Shags

Antarctic shags are part of the
cormorant family. Cormorants
are large diving birds. Antarctic
shags are the only cormorant
species to live in Antarctica.

The birds are often found living in **colonies** on packed ice. They do not **migrate**. However, they do move around to find open water to hunt in.

Antarctic shags usually weigh around 7 pounds (3.2 kg). They grow up to 30 inches (76 cm) long. Their **wingspans** can be more than 3 feet (0.9 m) long!

The birds are white and black
in color. The bright blue rings
around their eyes make them
easy to spot. They also have
yellowish growths at the base
of their beaks.

Hunting & Food

Antarctic shags hunt in groups. Hundreds of them sit on the water. They dive over and over to grab the fish swimming below.

Antarctic shags are great divers. They have been known to dive to depths of 380 feet (116 m). When the birds are underwater, they tuck in their wings. Their powerful **webbed** feet help **propel** them.

Baby Antarctic Shags

Couples build nests that are shaped like a volcano. Between October and December, females lay about 2 or 3 eggs. Chicks hatch after about 30 days. Their parents continue to care for them.

Males do most of the hunting and feeding. Females keep the chicks warm. After about 3 weeks, the chicks begin to grow their feathers. Soon, they will be ready to take on Antarctica!

More Facts

- Antarctic shags also go by king cormorants, blue-eyed shags, and a few other names.

- Antarctic shags use teamwork to hunt. Hunting in large groups can confuse fish. One bird can scare a fish into the mouth of another.

- The blue ring surrounding the Antarctic shag's eye is not a part of the eye. It is bright blue skin!

Glossary

colony – a group of animals of the same type living closely together.

migrate – to move from one place to another, usually for food or to have young.

propel – to cause to move forward.

species – a group of living things that look very much alike, share a similar name, and can have young with one another.

webbed – joined by skin.

wingspan – the distance from the tip of one wing of a bird to the tip of the other.

Index

Abdo Kids
ONLINE
FREE! ONLINE MULTIMEDIA RESOURCES

Visit **abdokids.com** to access crafts, games, videos, and more!

Use Abdo Kids code
AAK9384
or scan this QR code!